SELL LIKE CRAZY

Strategies To Boost Your Sales And Crush Competition.

Charles S. Breton

Table Of Contents:

INTRODUCTION:

If I had to sum up the core of this book in one sentence, it would be: "The quickest way to make money." I put this at the beginning of the book so I don't waste your time. I'm aware that this opening statement will be off-putting to many people, and I'd much rather they read another business book with all the usual platitudes like "follow your dreams," "work hard," "hire the right people," and so on. If that's what you're looking for, then just search Amazon. You'll find plenty of books on these topics, mostly written by professional authors and researchers who have never actually built a successful business.

This book is unapologetically about growing your business quickly and reaping the rewards of that kind of success.
Indeed, money isn't everything, but it's pretty darn close to oxygen in terms of importance. Without money, businesses don't last very long. That's why I'm so

focused on getting it. There are a few good reasons for this. To start, money can help you solve a lot of the problems that come with running a business. It's like a magic wand that can make a lot of the headaches go away.

Plus, when you have money, you can help others. If you're not in business to make money, then you're either not being honest or you're just doing it for fun. Sure, it's great to make a difference and all that, but how much of that can you do if you don't have any money? How many people can you help? It's like when you're on a plane and they go through all the safety procedures. The airline attendant will usually say something like this: "Put your oxygen mask on first before helping others." The same goes for money. Take care of yourself first, and then you can help others.

In the event of a sudden drop in cabin pressure, oxygen masks will be released from the ceiling above your seat. Put the mask over your face and pull the strap to secure it. If you are traveling with children or someone who needs help, make sure you put your mask on first before helping others.

Why assist others before putting on your mask? Because if you're hunched over your chair and in need of oxygen:
1. You can't help anyone else, and even worse;
2. We now have to deploy scarce resources to come and help you, otherwise you'll soon be dead.

You don't need the reflexes of a Grand Prix driver, the strength of Hercules, or the intelligence of Einstein to survive an impossible circumstance.

All you need to do is know what to do. The statistics vary on exactly what percentage of businesses fail within the first five years. Some estimates put it as high as 90%. However, I've never seen this statistic being quoted as anything less than 50%. That means that if we're being super-optimistic you have a 50 /50 chance of still having your doors open after five years.

But this is where things start to go south. Only businesses that entirely stop doing business are included in the data.

They ignore the fact that some firms plateau at a low level and gradually kill their owners or make their lives miserable.

Have you ever wondered why the majority of small businesses reach a plateau? It's quite common for small businesses to remain at the same level, only generating enough profit for the owner(s) to make a modest living. Despite their best efforts, they often find themselves stuck and frustrated. In this situation, one of two things usually happens: they become disheartened or they just accept that their business is nothing more than a low-paid, self-created job.

In reality, many business owners would be better off finding a job in their industry. This way, they would work fewer hours, have less stress, enjoy more benefits, and have more holiday time than in the 'prison' they have created for themselves. On the other hand, some business owners seem to have it all. They work reasonable hours, have a great cash flow from their business, and experience continuous growth. Business owners who are having a hard time often point the finger at their industry. Certain sectors are indeed on the decline - think bookstores and video rental stores. If you're in one of these industries that are no longer thriving, it may be time to accept the situation and move on, rather than draining yourself financially. This can be especially tough if you've been in the industry for a long time.

But, more often than not, people are just looking for someone to blame. I hear a lot of complaints about industries, such as:

- It's too competitive.
- The margins are too low.
- Online discounters are taking customers away.
- Advertising no longer works.

Since there are others in the same industry who are doing quite well, the industry is rarely the real culprit. What are they doing differently, then, is the obvious question.

Many proprietors of small businesses are caught in the trap. In other words, they are skilled technicians, such as plumbers, hairdressers, dentists, and others. They experience "entrepreneurial seizure" and begin to question whether they should continue to work for their foolish boss.

I'm skilled at what I do, so I'll launch my own company.

This is one of the **major mistakes** made by most small business owners. They move from having a stupid boss to being a stupid boss themselves! Here's the important thing: Just because you're good at what you do technically, doesn't guarantee you're good at what you do commercially.

So, returning to our earlier example, a talented plumber is not always the greatest candidate to manage a plumbing company. This crucial distinction should be noted since it plays a major role in why most small businesses fail. Although the business owner may possess exceptional technical talents, it is his lack of business skills that make his company fail.

This is not meant to discourage anyone from starting their own business. However, it's important to understand that business success requires more than just technical know-how. A business can be a great way to achieve financial freedom and personal satisfaction, but only if you understand the difference between the technical and business aspects and take the necessary steps to make your business successful. If you're confident in your technical skills but need help with the business side of things, then you're in luck. This book is designed to help you make sense of the business side of things and give you the tools you need to make your business a success.

Don't let yourself be the one who messes up. Having a plan can make a huge difference in the success of your business. It's like getting on a plane with a pilot who hasn't made a flight plan - you wouldn't do it, so why would you do the same with your business? The stakes are often high. It's more than just your ego on the line so it's time to "go pro" and create a plan.

CHAPTER ONE
MEANING OF MARKETING

Some people mistakenly believe that marketing is the same as branding, advertising, or some other nebulous idea. Even though they are all related to marketing, they are not the same thing.

Here is the clearest, most straightforward explanation of marketing you're ever going to read:

If you paint a sign proclaiming "Circus Coming to the Showground Saturday" and the circus is coming to town, that is *Advertising.*

Promotion occurs when a sign is carried into town on the back of an elephant.

Publicity would result from the elephant strolling through the mayor's flowerbed and a local newspaper article about it.

And if you get the mayor to laugh about it, that's **Public Relations.**

If the town's citizens go to the circus, you show them the many entertainment booths, explain how much fun they'll have spending money at the booths, answer their questions, and, ultimately, they spend a lot at the circus, **That's Sales.**
And if you planned the whole thing, that's **Marketing.**

Yup, it's as simple as that--marketing is the strategy you use for getting your ideal target market to know you, like you, and trust you enough to become a customer. All the stuff you usually associate with marketing is tactics. We'll talk more about strategy vs. tactics in a moment.
However, before we do that you need to understand that a fundamental shift has occurred in the last decade and things will never be the same.

A graduating class exam was once administered by Albert Einstein. It came out that the exam was the same as the one he had given them the year before. His teaching assistant was worried by what he observed and informed Einstein, believing it to be the consequence of the professor's forgetfulness.

The timid assistant, unsure of how to inform the great man of his error, stammered, "Excuse me, sir."
Einstein responded, "Yes."
It's concerning the test you just gave out, um, eh,"
Patiently, Einstein waited.
"I don't know if you realize it, but you gave this test last year. In actuality, it's the same.
After a brief period of reflection, Einstein said, Yes, the test is the same, but the answers have changed.

The solutions in business and marketing alter as discoveries are made, just as they do in physics. Once upon a time, all of your marketing for the year was accomplished by placing an advertisement in the Yellow Pages and paying them a boatload of cash. You now have to think about Google, social media, blogs, websites, and a plethora of other things. A whole new universe of rivals has emerged thanks to the internet.

Previously, your competition might have been down the street, but now they might be halfway over the world.

This causes many business owners trying to sell their brand to become immobilized by the "bright shiny object syndrome."

At this point, individuals tend to get sucked into the latest "hot" marketing strategies, such as video advertising.

They become preoccupied with methods and strategies rather than understanding the overall goal and rationale behind their actions.

COMPONENTS OF MARKETING

Writing a list of bullet points describing your anticipated output or goals for the upcoming weeks, months, or years is not enough to create a successful marketing strategy. You need to have a lot of reliable factors to concentrate on to promote effectively.

A marketing strategy is what?
An organized plan made to outline and direct marketing efforts to achieve particular results is known as a marketing strategy. It serves as the cornerstone for all marketing decisions. The main goal of a marketing strategy is to keep your marketing activities and objectives focused and in line with the overall business objectives.

Any effective marketing plan must take both internal and external elements into account. The marketing mix, performance evaluation, budgetary restrictions, etc. are examples of internal influences. The socioeconomic environment, competitor analysis, customer experience, and other aspects are examples of external influences. Because of this, the majority of marketing plans are both partially planned and partially market-reactive.

Having a general idea of what a marketing plan is is fine, but staying on top of your game requires that you understand and use the key elements that make up a solid strategy.
What Are The 5 Major Components of a Marketing Strategy?

1. Target Audience

The people who are most likely to identify with your brand and use your goods or services are referred to as your target audience. To convert leads and, of course, make a profit, you must identify your ideal audience.

Some companies use mass marketing, which means they aim for everyone. Use IKEA as an illustration. They offer flat-pack furniture, home furnishings, and appliances, and practically every customer can find the ideal product there. This tactic works so well because mass marketing is often only feasible for companies that sell items that are in high demand worldwide.

Most brands however will need to target several different audiences or concentrate on specific, niche groups of people for maximum success. To define, redefine, or re-establish your ideal target audience, you need to act on market segmentation.

There are four main types of market segmentation:
- Demographic (age, gender, income, marital status, etc.)
- Geographic (location, urbanicity, climate, culture, language)
- Psychographic (values, likes, dislikes, lifestyles, opinions, etc.)

- Behavioural (actions made within a website, in-app, in-store)

By conducting interviews, reviewing census data, developing online surveys, investigating social media analytics, examining the activities that clients and prospects take in your app or on your website, and other methods, you can gather demographic, geographic, psychographic, and behavioral data.

You can develop buyer personas (or redefine/re-establish them, if you have previously created some) after dynamically segmenting the data of your customers and prospects. A buyer persona is an imagined portrait of your ideal client that was developed using data. You assign these character attributes based on information about their age, income, touchpoints, pain areas, objectives, and purchasing habits. Making a persona (or several personas) is meant to give your meticulous audience targeting some structure.

Setting up buyer personas and putting market segmentation into practice gives your company a context in the real world. This will help with resource alignment, content production, product development, and learning more about your target customer. This kind of thorough audience research makes sure that your business message reaches the people who will benefit from it the most and provide value in return.

2. Goals & Objectives.

A goal is something you wish to accomplish; it's a big, all-encompassing statement that usually has a long time frame in mind. An objective involves the action or acts that will be conducted to accomplish the overall aim and is more definite, explicit, and detailed.

The SWOT analysis method is an excellent way to go deeper into your business (as well as the larger market environment) and identify some concrete goals and objectives if you feel a little lost or aren't sure where to start.

Conducting a SWOT analysis encourages you to identify your business and/or marketing strengths, weaknesses, opportunities, and threats. This will give you a clear picture of where you excel, where you can improve, your potential opportunities, and the challenges that you will need to tackle.

Consider the scenario where your marketing materials are getting a lot of attention and your marketing qualified leads (MQLs) are growing rapidly. Of course, this is a plus. Your MQLs are expanding, but they aren't converting, which is a concern. Getting leads that don't convert would be viewed as a drawback because marketing attempts to produce leads to expand your business. However, you may seize this opening by setting a goal to raise your MQL conversion rate for the following four quarters.

Here's an example of 3 clear-cut objectives that will help you achieve your new goal:

- Make a pillar page for the good or service you provide that has 20+ pieces of supporting material, such as blogs, infographics, videos, and instructions.

- Make fresh, product-focused website content that explains your product or service's features and advantages in detail.

- For the emails that performed the worst, analyze and rewrite your workflows to include new content and additional product-focused details.

Of course, your goals and the tasks you must complete to get there do not have to be as significant or last a full year as in the aforementioned example. You can make them as extensive or as simple as you want.

Having strong goals and objectives is super important for any business, regardless of company size, budget, or offerings. The focus of your goals and objectives can be to inform your content, explore different avenues with your social media, bridge the gap between sales and marketing, increase email open rates, improve lead quality, etc.

A key thing to remember here is to ensure that your goals and objectives are **S.M.A.R.T.:**

- Specific
- Measurable
- Achievable
- Relevant/realistic
- Time-bound

The general goal of creating goals and objectives in your marketing plan is to attain business aims as smoothly as possible, whether that means focusing on revenue, increasing your brand, or entering new markets.

3. Competitor Analysis.

Competitor analysis is a procedure where you research to find companies that could pose a threat to your enterprise and evaluate their goods, sales, marketing methods, online presence on social media, websites, etc. By performing a competitor analysis, you will learn about and comprehend:

- The market you operate within
- Your target audience
- Market forecasting and potential opportunities
- Competitor products & product development horizons
- Pricing structures
- Acquisition trends

This gives you a clear picture of where you stand to competitors and a benchmark by which to gauge the expansion of your company. It will be simpler to spot prospective possibilities and areas where you can outperform and surpass them to acquire an advantage the more you get to know your opponent. Studying your market competitors can therefore not only enable you to maintain your position as the leader but will also broaden your understanding of the kind of marketing that is effective and ineffective in your sector. To acquire a competitive edge, 90% of Fortune 500 organizations already employ competitive intelligence.

Side note: No matter how specialized your brand, product, or service is, you will always have a competition to deal with. You will inevitably run across rivalry in some element of your business, even if it's indirect. This competition could simply be other places where potential consumers are spending their money, using social media, or reading blogs with material that is similar to yours.

You must convey the unique attributes of your brand and the reasons why prospects and customers should select you over competing products. You need to follow a few particular procedures and make use of the available resources to do a full, useful competition analysis; doing so requires more than simply a simple Google search.

4. Content Creation.

The development of content is a crucial component of contemporary marketing. Why? Because modern marketing involves more than just obtrusive promotional strategies and blatant advertisements. With effective content marketing, you can convince your target audience that you are competent, reliable, and capable of providing them with the benefits they seek.

According to research, 70% of marketers said they were actively spending money on content marketing. This is because the material on a brand's website today serves as much more than simply a slogan or a promotional piece; it also serves as a business strategy that aims to establish thought leadership, attract an audience, encourage conversion, keep customers loyal, and much more.

Content marketing comes in many forms, including (but not limited to):

- Blogs
- Infographics
- Videos
- Guides
- Podcasts

There is a distinction between material that is valuable and information that is there merely for the sake of it, even though the influence of content marketing is expanding year over year. A poorly targeted or insufficiently researched piece of writing or media won't be able to convert leads. Such material will come across as amateurish, wasteful for the viewer, and potentially damaging to your business. A fantastic method to make sure the material you produce is worthwhile, helpful to your target audience, and competitive on Search Engine Results Pages (SERPs) is to construct a

Search Insights Report (S.I.R.) A search insights report serves as a guide for your content development and is essentially a cross between a keyword research report and a content calendar.

If you have never conducted a search insights report, here's a quick rundown of the things you need to do:

1. Select Your Focus Topics: these should be based on the product or service you provide and they act as your main keywords (for example, with Hurree, one of our main topics is 'Market Segmentation' and another is 'Marketing Strategy').

2. Run A Content Competitor Analysis: Once you've determined who your content rivals are, it's time to research them using a keyword tool to see which search terms they may be ranking for that your site may not be. Many excellent tools are accessible, like Ahrefs, SEMrush, and

Moz. Alternatively, you might try The Hoth, which is cost-free for a specific set of keywords. You should get a big list of topic-specific keywords after adding your content rivals to the keyword research tool of your choice.

If a keyword is appropriate for your audience and doesn't have a lot of competition (you can tell by looking at the monthly search volume, or MSV), you can regard it as a potential piece of content. A score of 50 to 1000 monthly searches is considered decent or attainable. It will be harder to rank if you're attempting to do so for a keyword with an MSV of 25K.

STRATEGY VS TACTICS

Success in marketing depends largely on being able to distinguish between strategy and tactics. The broad preparation you perform before the tactics is your strategy. Consider purchasing an empty piece of property to build a home. Would you simply place a brick order and begin placing the bricks? Not. The result would be a huge mess that probably wasn't safe.

What then do you choose to do? The first thing you do is engage a builder and an architect, and they plan out everything for you—from the important details, like obtaining building licenses, to the specific tap fittings you want. Before a single shovel of earth is lifted, all of this has been planned. That is strategy.

Once you have a plan in place, you can determine how many bricks you'll need, where to put the foundation, and what kind of roof you'll have. A bricklayer, carpenter, plumber, electrician, and other professionals are now available for hire. That is tactics.

Without both strategy and tactics, you cannot do anything worthwhile successfully. Without tactics, a strategy results in analytical paralysis. No matter how talented the builder and architect are, the house won't be constructed until the bricks are laid. They will eventually have to say, "Okay, the blueprint is now good. Let's get started since we have all the necessary approvals for construction.

Without a strategy, tactics can result in "bright shiny object syndrome." Imagine that you began constructing a wall without any designs and later discovered that it was in the incorrect location. You then begin pouring the foundation and discover that it is improper for this type of house. Next, you begin excavating the area for the pool, only to discover that this is also improper. This won't work. Yet many business owners do conduct their marketing in this way. They combine a variety of haphazard strategies in the hopes that one of them would result in a client.

They throw together a website hastily and it turns out to be an online version of their brochure, or they start advertising on social media because they've heard it's the newest thing, etc.

Both strategy and tactics are necessary for success, but strategy must come first since it determines the techniques you employ. Here's where your marketing strategy comes into play. Consider your marketing strategy to be the blueprint for attracting and keeping clients.

CHAPTER TWO

UNDERSTANDING YOUR TARGET AUDIENCE

Customers control the purchasing process, thus marketers that want to stand out from the flood of competing brands and advertisements must provide customers with focused, individualized experiences. Marketers can choose media, messaging, and timing more wisely when they have a thorough understanding of their target customers. Let's examine what a target audience is in detail and the measures you may take to identify yours:

What Is a Target Audience?
The particular set of people you wish to reach with your marketing message is known as a target audience. They are the people who are most likely to purchase your goods or services, and they share some traits like behaviors and demographics.

You may better grasp how and where to contact your ideal potential clients by properly defining your target market. To get the best conversion rates, you can start with general categories like millennials or single fathers, but you need to get far more specific than that. Don't be reluctant to be specific. This is all about properly focusing your marketing efforts, not discouraging customers from purchasing your goods.

Even though they are not the primary focus of your marketing plan, customers who are not the target of your focused advertising might nonetheless make purchases from you. Although you can't sell to everyone, you can target some people.

Research, not intuition, should be used to determine your target audience. Even if they aren't the clients you first set out to attract, you need to go after the ones who want to buy from you.

Target audiences center around a specific group of people. These can be men, women, teenagers, or children. They generally share an interest such as reading, running, or soccer. Personas can help advertisers investigate relevant magazine titles or industry publications.

Understanding your target audience is essential for marketers. Every marketing strategy and plan you employ will be defined by this information. Although airing an advertisement could seem like a terrific approach to reach as many people as possible, it is also costly. Additionally, only 25% of the views would be genuine buyers of your product. Your advertisement will be seen by fewer, but the correct, individuals if you know that your target audience reads a particular publication or watches a particular program. If you sell running shoes, for instance, adverts in running periodicals may be more appropriate for reaching your target market. Choosing the appropriate media is crucial to the success of your marketing campaigns.

Understanding your target market not only improves success but also enables you to interact with customers more effectively. You can create content that appeals to particular personas and create brands that reflect the preferences and ideals of individuals who are most likely to buy the product. This is crucial at a time when consumers demand every advertisement to be extremely targeted and individualized. 80% of consumers claim that tailored encounters increase their likelihood of doing business with a brand.

KINDS OF TARGET AUDIENCE

In marketing, identifying and understanding the target audience is crucial for crafting effective marketing strategies. There are various types of target audiences, and each requires a unique approach. Here are some common types of target audiences:

Interest:
Group people into various interests, such as hobbies and entertainment choices, and then divide them into different groups. This can assist you in creating data-driven, highly tailored communications that enable you to engage with your audience and foster brand loyalty.

Buying Intention:
Describe the types of people who are looking for particular products, such as new cars or entertainment systems. Understanding your audience's problems will enable you to

develop a message that is specific to their needs.

Subcultures:

Subcultures refer to groups of people who share a common experience, such as music genres or entertainment fandoms. By understanding some of your target audience's motivations, you can better understand who you're trying to connect with.

Behavioral Target Audience:

This audience is segmented based on their past behaviors, such as purchase history, online interactions, brand loyalty, and engagement. Analyzing behavior helps businesses predict future actions and design targeted campaigns.

Understanding these various types of target audiences empowers marketers to create personalized and relevant marketing campaigns. By tailoring messages, content, and promotions to specific groups, businesses can increase engagement, conversion rates, and overall marketing success.

Note:

A target market is the set of consumers that a company plans to sell to or reach with marketing activities. A target audience is a group or segment within that target market that is being served advertisements. This makes the target audience a more specific subset of a target market. The target audience can often be used interchangeably with the target market, as it is a specific subset of the largest market group.

WAYS TO DETERMINE YOUR TARGET AUDIENCE

To determine your target audience, you must spend time analyzing the data you receive from consumer engagements, evaluating current buyers and purchase trends, and optimizing as new information is revealed.

The following steps should help you realize your target audience:

1. Analyze Your Customer Base and Carry Out Client Interviews;

Examining the people who have already purchased your goods or services is one of the finest ways to identify your target market. What are their age, places of residence, and areas of interest? Engaging in social media activity or sending customer surveys are effective ways to find out this information.

2. Conduct Market Research and Identify Industry Trends!

To identify service gaps that your product can solve, look at the market research for your sector. Focus more on your product's distinctive qualities after looking at trends for comparable items to determine where they are putting their efforts.

3. Analyze Competitors;

Marketers can learn a lot by looking at competitors to see who they are commonly selling to, and how they go about it. Are they using online or offline channels? Are they focusing on the decision-maker or the supporter?

4. Create Personas;

An excellent technique to hone in on the various groups that make up your target audience is to create personas. This is particularly useful if your product appeals to a broad range of buyers. You can use personas to identify the broad demographics, characteristics, and demands of your target audience. Personas are developed using data from surveys, digital interactions, and other sources that marketers can use to get a more complete picture of the target market. Favorite pastimes, television shows, magazines, etc. may fall under this category. Marketing professionals are advised to create three to five personas.

5. Define Who Your Target Audience Isn't;

There will certainly be consumers who are close to your target demographic, but who will not act on messaging. Try to be specific in determining who your audience is and who it isn't. Is your demographic women, or women between the ages of 20 and 40? Knowing this will keep your teams from devoting ad dollars to segments that will not yield returns.

6. Continuously Revise;

You will get a more precise understanding of your target audiences as you acquire more information and engage with clients. Based on this knowledge, you must continually refine and enhance personas to get the greatest outcomes.

7. Utilize Google Analytics;

Google Analytics provides a wealth of information about the people who visit your website. Making more data-driven decisions during the media planning process will enable you to identify critical insights such as the channels your target audience is using or the types of content they connect and engage with most.

The target audience in marketing offers several advantages:

Enhanced Communication:

By adjusting your messages and communication style to better suit your target audience, you may increase the likelihood that they will engage.

Efficient Resource Allocation:
You may allocate your marketing budget more effectively and stop spending money on people who aren't interested in what you have to say by concentrating on a certain audience.

Product Development Improvements:
The likelihood of success rises when products or services are designed to better satisfy the wants and preferences of your target audience.

Higher Conversion Rates:
Because you are targeting their particular interests and pain areas when you target a specific audience, your marketing efforts have a higher chance of converting leads into customers.

Brand Loyalty:
Strong relationships with your target market encourage brand loyalty because they feel heard and supported by your business.

Competitive Benefit:
Knowing who your target market is can help you stand out from the crowd by developing value propositions that are specifically tailored to them.

Data-Driven Decision Making:
Making informed judgments is facilitated by gathering and evaluating data on your target market, allowing you to continuously improve your marketing tactics.

Enhanced ROI
You may expect greater returns on your marketing investments if you concentrate on the correct demographic because you will be more likely to draw in qualified leads and clients.

Personalization Opportunities:
Enhancing customer experiences is made possible by personalizing marketing messaging based on audience analytics.

Adaptability and Growth
Understanding your target market can help you modify your marketing initiatives to reflect shifting preferences and trends, enabling sustainable growth as your business develops.

To effectively interact and connect with potential customers, keep in mind that the success of a marketing strategy heavily depends on identifying and understanding the target demographic.

MEANING OF DIGITAL MARKETING

What Is Digital Marketing?

The term digital marketing refers to the use of digital channels to market products and services to consumers. This type of marketing involves the use of websites, mobile devices, social media, search engines, and other similar channels. Digital marketing became popular with the advent of the Internet in the 1990s.

Digital marketing is frequently seen as an additional strategy by businesses to reach customers and comprehend their behavior. It has some of the same ideas as traditional marketing. Traditional and digital marketing strategies are frequently combined by businesses. However, unconscious prejudice is one of the unique issues that face digital marketing.

Marketing to consumers via digital channels, including websites, mobile apps, and social media platforms, is known as digital marketing.

Internet marketing, which only takes place on websites, is distinct from this type of marketing.

Digital marketing deals with luring clients using email, content marketing, search engines, social media, and other channels.

How to stand out in a world that is overrun with digital marketing advertisements is one of the main issues that digital marketers confront.

Implicit bias is one of several problems with digital marketing.

How Digital Marketing Works;

Marketing refers to activities that a company uses to promote its products and services and to improve its market share. To be successful, it requires a combination of advertising savvy, sales, and the ability to deliver goods to end-users. Professionals, known as marketers, take on these tasks either internally at companies or externally at marketing firms.

Traditionally, businesses concentrated their marketing efforts on print, television, and radio. These choices are still available, but the Internet caused a change in how businesses interact with their customers. Digital marketing became useful in this situation. Websites, social media, search engines, and apps—anything that combines marketing with consumer feedback or a two-way connection between the business and its customers—are all used in this type of marketing.

New technologies and trends forced companies to change their marketing strategies. Email became a popular marketing tool in the early days of digital marketing. Then, the focus shifted to search engines like Netscape, which allowed businesses to tag and keyword items to get themselves noticed. The development of sites like Facebook made it possible for companies to track data and cater to consumer trends.

Nowadays, businesses can sell themselves, their goods and services, and themselves to consumers more easily thanks to smartphones and other digital gadgets. People prefer utilizing their phones to access the internet, according to studies. A Pew Research Center research found that more than 75% of American adults frequently use their phones when shopping.

Digital marketing can be interactive and is often used to target specific segments of the customer base (Sources and Receivers).

Advertisers are commonly referred to as sources, while recipients of the targeted ads are the receivers. Sources frequently target highly specific, well-defined receivers.

TYPES OF DIGITAL MARKETING CHANNELS

As noted above, marketing was traditionally done through print (newspapers and magazines) and broadcast ads (TV and radio). These channels still exist and are used today. Digital marketing channels have evolved and continue to do so. The following are eight of the most common digital avenues that companies can take to boost their marketing efforts. Keep in mind that some companies may use multiple channels in their efforts.

Website Marketing

All digital marketing efforts revolve around a website. It is a very effective channel on its own, but it also serves as the platform for several different web marketing efforts. A website ought to convey a brand, a product, and a service understandably and memorably. It must be quick, responsive, and simple to use.

Pay-Per-Click Advertising

Pay-per-click (PPC) advertising enables marketers to reach internet users on several digital platforms through paid ads. Marketers can set up PPC campaigns on Google, Bing, LinkedIn, Twitter, Pinterest, and Facebook and show their ads to people searching for terms related to products or services.

These ads can target users specifically based on their hobbies or geography, or segment users based on demographic traits (including age or gender). The two most widely used PPC systems are Google Ads and Facebook Ads.

Content Marketing

Reaching potential customers by using content that appeals to them is the aim of content marketing. The typical process for promoting content is to put it on a website and then use social media, email marketing, search engine optimization, or even pay-per-click campaigns. Blogs, ebooks, online courses, infographics, podcasts, and webinars are some of the content marketing tools.

Email Marketing

One of the most successful digital marketing methods is still email marketing. Email marketing is not the same as spam email, although many people think it is. Companies can connect with prospective customers and anybody else interested in their brands and products with this sort of marketing.

Many digital marketers add leads to their email lists using all other digital marketing methods. They then develop client acquisition funnels employing email marketing to convert those prospects into paying customers.

Social Media Marketing

A social media marketing campaign's main objectives are to increase brand recognition and foster interpersonal trust. As you learn more about social media marketing, you can employ it as a channel for direct marketing or sales as well as lead generation. Twitter and promoted posts are two instances of social media marketing.

Affiliate Marketing

One of the earliest types of marketing is affiliate marketing, and the internet has given it new life. Influencers who use affiliate marketing to promote other people's products are paid every time a lead or sale is generated. Millions of dollars are paid out each month to websites that sell products from numerous well-known corporations, including Amazon, through their affiliate programs.

Video Marketing

One of the most well-known search engines in the world is YouTube. Before making a purchase decision, many internet users visit YouTube to learn something new, read a review, or just unwind.

To launch a video marketing campaign, marketers can choose from a variety of platforms, such as Facebook Videos, Instagram, and TikTok. Integrating video into SEO, content marketing, and more extensive social media marketing efforts helps businesses use it most effectively.

SMS Messaging

Companies and nonprofit groups utilize text messaging, also known as SMS or short message service, to tell clients about upcoming sales or to provide them with possibilities. SMS marketing campaigns are another tool used by candidates for political offices to promote their platforms. With the development of technology, many text-to-give initiatives now enable donors to make a direct payment or contribution by sending a short text message.

BENEFITS OF DIGITAL MARKETING

The dominant marketing tactic of the twenty-first century is digital marketing, and in years to come the global market for it will be worth billions of dollars. However, not all businesses have adopted this marketing approach. Despite the widespread use of digital marketing, some businesses continue to rely on traditional marketing tactics or only dabble in it, spending too little time and money to have a significant influence.

Understanding the advantages of digital marketing could increase its influence on your company, which could ultimately lead to missed opportunities for growth. Understanding the most prevalent benefits of digital marketing will put you in a strong position to create a winning plan and make wise investments in successful digital marketing initiatives.

In this article, we'll explain the most common benefits of digital marketing for businesses today and why it's so important to create a thoughtful strategy. Whether you're starting from scratch or refining your existing strategy, it's a good time to review your plan and make sure it's designed to maximize the key benefits.

Below are the most common benefits of digital marketing, including:
- Global reach
- Cost efficiency
- Measurable results
- Effective targeting
- Increased engagement
- Flexibility
- Improved conversion rate
- Social currency
- Greater ROI

1. Global Reach

The geographic scope of conventional marketing techniques like billboards, TV commercials, and cold calls is constrained. However, with the help of digital marketing, companies may reach customers in all countries and time zones. You can target potential clients in your state, country, or even the entire world rather than just those in your local town.

Traditional marketing strategies could be very expensive for businesses to use to advertise themselves in numerous areas. It's simple for businesses to connect with potential customers all around the world thanks to digital media methods like social media, content marketing, and email marketing. You may easily scale up your efforts to develop your brand and boost sales if you have a wider pool of potential clients.

2. Cost Efficiency

Marketers succeed when they're good stewards of their budgets. Fortunately, investing in digital marketing can make the most of even a modest budget.

For example, a typical print ad can cost upward of $2,000 — and it's also difficult to measure the precise number of sales generated as a result of a print ad, even with tactics like unique tracking links or QR codes. Modern strategies like email marketing can help businesses generate an average of $42 for every $1 spent.

The majority of digital marketing techniques are inexpensive to launch. For instance, some of the best methods for online business promotion include search engine optimization (SEO), social networking, and content marketing, all of which require little more than your time and effort.

Digital channels typically don't have minimum budget restrictions for search engine marketing (SEM) campaigns or social media ad purchases, even on the paid marketing front. Regardless of your spending limit, you may design a campaign that is exactly targeted to your potential clients while staying within your budget.

3. Measurable Results
Results from digital marketing are quantifiable.

Digital marketing is not only more economical than offline marketing strategies, but it is also more measurable. While traditional media like print, TV, and radio advertisements might be beneficial, it can be quite difficult to determine who is responding to your messaging.

You can virtually track every interaction a person has with your business using digital marketing. Every facet of digital marketing can be closely monitored, whether it be viewed on social media, clicks on ads, email opens, or organic page views. As a result, it is much simpler to demonstrate the return on investment (ROI) of your digital marketing efforts, which aids in your understanding of the outcomes you are producing and where to continue investing.

4. Effective Targeting

You have limited control over who sees your material when using traditional marketing. You can't be certain that everyone reading a specialist publication is your ideal buyer, even if you pay for a tailored advertisement there.

However, using online audiences and targeting data, digital marketing enables you to identify the optimum audience for your communications. Data from your digital marketing can also be gathered to determine which types of customers respond best to particular types of content. These insights can assist you in adjusting your campaigns over time if you're still getting to know the preferences of your clients.

5. Increased Engagement

Only one-way interactions are possible with traditional marketing strategies. There is no obvious way for your audience to instantly respond or take action to the message that your business is trying to convey to them. This creates a barrier between your brand and the target market, which may result in lower engagement.

You have the chance to engage in actual interactions with your customers through digital marketing. At every step of the process, you may collect feedback from your clients via email, SMS, social media, or blog comments. This increases your options to please customers, respond to their inquiries, and improve your efforts in light of their feedback. It helps that these interactions give you more opportunities to interact with customers, which can boost conversions and sales.

6. Flexibility

Digital marketing gives you the flexibility to choose from different channels and strategies
. It's also flexible enough that you can adjust your approach over time as you learn more about what works for your audience and business.

CHAPTER THREE

CRAFTING AN EFFECTIVE MARKET STRATEGY

Effective marketing can bring a whole host of benefits to your business. In light of this, let's examine all you should understand about developing a marketing strategy.

Getting your goods and/or services in front of customers may be an exciting challenge, whether you're a small business owner or a member of a larger marketing team. Knowing how to appeal to your target market requires a wide range of abilities and expertise, and developing a marketing strategy might be crucial.

We take a closer look at exactly what a marketing strategy is, as well as why you need one. We also explore what you need to develop an effective strategy and the steps you need to take to do so.

What is a marketing strategy?

First, let's examine what exactly we mean by the word "marketing strategy." It appears to be a fairly simple idea at first glance—a way to describe how you approach marketing and sales. However, in practice, the idea is more nuanced.

A few helpful definitions are floating around, upon closer study. One of the best definitions of a marketing strategy comes from Investopedia, which describes it as "a business's overall game plan for reaching prospective consumers and turning them into customers of the products or services the business provides."

So, it's about strategic planning on how you're going to get your business in front of the people who are going to buy from it. As we'll see, there are many facets to this process, with a lot of analysis, preparation, and research.

Why do I need one?

There are various reasons why you need a marketing strategy for your company. Without spending the time to develop a marketing strategy, your sales and promotional efforts will ultimately be less successful. This is due to several factors, many of which are essential for expanding your company:

It Assists You In Locating Your Intended Market.

Having a marketing strategy in place can help you connect with the proper individuals, which is one of the key reasons. Understanding your target audience is essential to success, as we discussed in our series on how to launch a business. When you have a marketing strategy in place, you can determine who your customers are, what they want from your business, and how to contact them.

It Aids You In Making Wise Financial Decisions.

When attempting to engage with your clients, there are many marketing avenues from which to select. Digital marketing choices like social media, content marketing, and email marketing are available in addition to more conventional techniques like print and TV advertising. Making a marketing strategy will help you decide where to spend your money on advertising to get the best results.

It Maintains Consistency In Your Marketing.

Consistency is crucial when attempting to expand your brand and attract new clients. Each channel's brand language and aesthetics should be consistent with your company's overall branding. This congruence is made possible by a marketing plan, which also ensures that the message you convey is understandable.

You Get A Quantified Result From It.

Setting goals is aided by developing a marketing plan. Once these are established, you can begin gauging the success of your initiatives. Having this knowledge can help you hone and enhance your marketing, whether for KPIs like ROI, engagement, or conversion rate.

It Serves As A Manual.

You have a detailed plan for how to interact with customers once you have a marketing strategy in place. You are aware of their buyer personas, their problems, and the best ways to communicate with them. This helps guide any team or individual at your organization who wishes to sell your goods or services.

HOW TO DEVELOP AN EFFECTIVE MARKETING STRATEGY

Planning and strategy go hand in hand in marketing. Making a plan follows developing a marketing strategy, and neither is complete or useful without the other. A corporation needs to seek both inside and internationally for both. You must understand both your brand and your target audience to create connections between the two.

We've described some of the actions you may follow when creating a marketing strategy and plans to assist you in getting started. These can be used as a starting point while working alone, even though the specific stages frequently vary depending on the organization.

1. Start With A Goal

The objectives of your marketing strategy should line up with those of your entire firm. For instance, if increasing income is your primary goal, your marketing plan goal can be to boost website traffic and conversions by a given percentage.

Creating a mission statement is another way to get started. This is essentially the "what" and "how" of your company—a description of your goals and your plan for achieving them. It can assist you in creating a central theme for your marketing initiatives, although being less measurable from an internal standpoint.

2. Do Your Marketing Analysis.

Understanding the market you'll be operating in is a prerequisite for creating a marketing strategy. Every stage of this procedure revolves around marketing analytics. However, you should first gain a sense of the existing circumstances both inside and internationally.

Pay attention to your business advantages and disadvantages, as well as recent market trends. Look for new and existing trends, then think about how you may profit from them. Try to draw attention to any difficulties that you, your rivals, or both may be experiencing.

3. Know Your Customers.

When you're planning, your customers should be the focus of everything you do. You must consider their wants and how you might meet them more successfully than your rivals while developing a marketing strategy.

You should start by identifying some of your target markets and taking your client personas into mind. These are two of the primary methods you may get to know and understand your clients, whether you're beginning a new business or are a part of an old one. By knowing the finer details of who you're trying to appeal to, you can then start to think about how you can go about doing so. It helps to make your marketing more targeted and relevant, increasing its chances of success.

4. Know Your Product And Resources.

Whether you have an established product/service or you're in the development stage, you need to have an understanding of what you'll be offering your customers. Your goal here is to understand your position in the market/industry.

There is a fairly well-established technique you can use at this stage, known as the '4 Ps of the marketing mix'. These four points are:

Product: Here, you should consider what you offer to customers and what makes it special. Consider whether it satisfies your clients' needs and whether there are any features you can add.

Price: This pertains to the price you charge for the goods and how it stacks up against your competitors, as one might assume. Consider ways to grow your market share as well, such as through marketing.

Promotion: What will most appeal to your audience and where can you promote your product? You should think about these issues as well as how these promotions fit into your brand identity.

Place: Finally, you need to consider where your product/service will be sold. Is it online only? Or do you have physical stores to think about? How easy is it for customers to navigate these? And who will distribute your product?

The 4 Ps can give you a firmer understanding of the products and resources you have available when it comes to marketing.

5. Further Define Your Objectives.

As said in step one, you should already have some overarching objectives for your company. You're going to need to be strategic if you want to accomplish this goal. Before achieving your main goal, you should consider some of the smaller goals you can accomplish.

As with many of the things mentioned here, your particular business will have a big impact on what the precise goals are. However, a few instances are:

- Gaining new customers
- Increasing sales or conversion rates
- Increasing brand awareness and engagement
- Growing your emailing list

You'll want to put measurable goals besides these. For example, one objective could be 'adding 2,000 new subscribers to the email list by the end of the year'. Remember, these should be SMART goals – specific, measurable, achievable, relevant, and timely.

6. Outline Techniques.

You should consider some of the marketing strategies and channels that are available after you have set and defined your goals. Again, these will mostly depend on your unique business and aims, and you can choose from a wide range of various approaches and technologies.

Let's use the aforementioned email subscription goal as an illustration. You might wish to consider strategies like boosting website traffic via social media marketing. Similarly to this, you might wish to increase the number of subscription calls to action in your content strategy. Then, you may use marketing analytics to emphasize the factors that are currently influencing your subscription rate.

7. Set A Budget.

Whether this point belongs in your marketing strategy or marketing plan is up for debate. Wherever you decide to incorporate it, though, it is a crucial step in the procedure. Make sure you have budgeted enough money to accomplish your goals without going overboard. Similarly to that, you must make sure that your investment is yielding a significant return for the marketing activity to be profitable.

Budgeting topics were covered in one of our posts on how to launch a business. Here, we stressed the significance of precisely estimating your return and costing your expenses. The same guidelines also apply here.

8. Analyze Performance.

Having a thorough method of monitoring performance is crucial, just like it is with almost every other aspect of running a firm.

When creating your marketing plans, you must consider how you will evaluate the performance of your efforts.

You can learn more about many other aspects of your marketing, in addition to things like web analytics. In the end, you'll need to apply this information to evaluate and enhance your marketing plan.

DO'S AND DON'TS OF A MARKETER

Communication and relationship-building with prospective clients and reference sources are key components of marketing your professional services. It necessitates a fundamental comprehension of strategies that typically yield positive results as well as strategies that don't.

Use this simple checklist of "do's and don'ts" to determine whether you are marketing your psychology practice correctly and avoiding problems.

DO;

1. Get your marketing materials such as your business card, brochure, and website in front of people and their hands. People aren't looking for your materials — you need to actively provide the information.

2. Stay up to date with changes and best practices for professional marketing copy online and offline to provide your audience with high-quality content that will keep them coming back. As your customers search for your goods and services online, use your content to address their inquiries.

3. Market your practice using terms that potential clients and referral sources understand. For example, avoid saying in your marketing materials that you "provide psychotherapeutic services for people whose psychosocial functioning is clinically impaired by their depressed mood, hypersomnia, and psychomotor retardation." Consider instead saying something like, "Are you feeling down in the dumps most days? Have you lost interest in things that you used to enjoy? Do you find that you are sleeping more than usual and having a hard time getting out of bed in the morning? If these problems are interfering with your work, school, family, or social life, you may be depressed. We can help."

4. Make use of social media to help your content reach your target audience. Select media outlets that appeal to your target market.

5. Focus on the benefits of your services. Instead of presenting a detailed description of what you do, your marketing materials should talk about how your services can help prospective clients.

6. Identify your unique professional strengths and use them as "selling points."

7. Build relationships with other professionals who interact with people in your target market — for example, lawyers, judges, and law enforcement officials, if you do forensics, work.

8. Observe how your competitors market similar services. Use the things that work and learn from their mistakes to market your practice more effectively.

9. Measure the effectiveness of your marketing efforts. It's crucial to monitor your progress whether you gather feedback informally by speaking with referral sources, coworkers, and community members or formally through focus groups, questionnaires, and other market research methods.

10. Consider including a question about how new clients heard about your practice on forms you use to collect information at intake.

DON'T;

1. Base your marketing efforts on untested assumptions. Use market research and planning in getting to know your client base and target market.

2. Become irrelevant. Keep an eye out for trends in your field and the environment, determine the talents that will become more and more crucial, and begin learning associated skills.

3. Assume you are an expert in marketing. Learn as much as you can about marketing your services effectively and know when you need to use consultants.

4. Don't plagiarize, copy, steal, or borrow other people's content. You can link or refer to it.

5. Don't act as if you have all the answers. Provide your expertise and ask for feedback.

6. Stop marketing. Marketing is an investment and the rewards accumulate over time.

7. Get discouraged by competition. It is advantageous for both the market and psychology, provided that psychologists develop the commercial skills necessary to compete successfully.

8.Don't create worthless, fluff content. Create valuable and helpful products that people will need.

9. Shortchange your marketing efforts. Make sure you budget adequately for them.

10. Offer services that clients don't value. No one will seek them, even if you market the services well.

IN SUMMARY:

- The small things in business trump the large things. What I'm trying to say is that there are a lot of tiny, annoying things in your business that are continuously clamoring for your attention, but these aren't the activities that generate income.

- Your attention as the creator of a company that you want to scale must shift from carrying out routine tasks to generating income and managing the ship.

- Selling should be your top concern as a business owner, and you must act as such. This entails focusing the majority of your time on tasks linked to marketing and sales.

- The market doesn't pay you to have the best products or services. It rewards you for solving problems.

- 'Why won't anybody listen to me?' It was from pondering this question that I had my first breakthrough. While it might seem obvious, I realized that nobody cared about me, my product, or anything else I was babbling about on the phone. They cared only about themselves!... I quickly found the more the call focused on solving their problem, the more sales I made.

- The deepest aspirations, pains, anxieties, hopes, and goals of your market and your prospects should be your main emphasis. You must understand them more thoroughly than any of your rivals before creating marketing messaging that clearly explains how you can address these issues.

- Following the creation of a list of these crucially important revenue-generating operations, it is time to set to work automating and developing solutions for the majority of the remaining tasks.

www.ingramcontent.com/pod-product-compliance
Lightning Source LLC
Chambersburg PA
CBHW062234290526
45794CB00006B/2284

* 9 7 9 8 8 5 4 3 0 1 8 3 1 *